Walls and Boxes

Contents

Foreword

Born in Dublin in 1952, Mark Guard emigrated to Canada in 1973. He charmingly admitted that his first enthusiasm then was to be an automotive designer and to train in Coventry, but this was discouraged by his parents. Not deterred, he rather surprisingly attended the School of Architecture at the University of Toronto during one of its more turbulent periods. Our paths crossed then. The conflict was based on the rediscovery of the pleasure of drawing and the investigation of previous solutions by many students, which were openly discouraged by the theoretical position of the school. There were moments, however, at the University of Toronto when preoccupations with the 'friendly object', the legacy of AS Neill's Summerhill and the Dutch structuralists (Aldo van Eyck and Herman Hertzberger) were influential.

Mark recrossed the Atlantic in 1979 to enrol in the emerging school of architecture at the Royal College of Art in London under John Miller and Kenneth Frampton's direction.

What had been a school of interior design, given prominence in the immediate post-Festival era by Hugh Casson, had become a school of architecture manqué. The school later received RIBA recognition in 1982. In opposition to the anti-architecture of the University of Toronto, case studies to Paris were organised to visit the Arcades, the Maison de Verre, the work of Mallet-Stevens and Le Corbusier. Frequent visits to Amsterdam and Utrecht also introduced students to the work of Duiker and Rietveld, and later the work of Terragni in Como. The unfinished business of the Heroic period of Modern architecture, interrupted by the Second World War, was under review and openly encouraged as part of the curriculum. And so Mark's early architectural beginnings were exposed to two diametrically opposed positions, but both passionately held.

The 1970s, in parallel, was an inventive period in London's domestic architecture, characterised by housing for the London boroughs, and in particular the example of Neave Brown at the London Borough of Camden. The cynicism of later years had not yet arrived. Today's residential design is unfortunately segregated commercially into inside and outside, between shell and core and interior design.

As an exemplar, the practice of the late Rick Mather should also be mentioned. Mark worked with Rick for three years and in many respects, this 'quiet American' was his mentor. Rick came from Oregon, bringing with him an infectious sense of style and sophistication—a flashback to Arlington Road, Camden Town in the early 1970s where he inverted the London terrace house and produced a remarkable and unexpected roof garden, double-height spaces and sanded floorboards, and furnished it with Thonet bentwood chairs and nineteenth-century city plans on the white walls. A similar palette would find itself in later diverse projects, from restaurants to Oxford colleges and national galleries and museums. Rick was the consummate designer.

And so this book and the example of Mark and his partners, Keith Tillman and Steven Pollock, comes as a timely rebuke to the negative tendencies of specialism and a reminder that quality only results with more inclusive design. Whether house, loft, or apartment, there is here an optimising of volume and dimension frequently liberating restrictive situations. This is a call to intelligence and the senses—games of the unexpected, beautifully concealed sliding doors allowing for generous spatial transformations, daylight from above illuminating the daily ritual of the shower, a mild obsession with gadgetry (and light switches in particular), a garden suddenly makes an appearance on the roof, a front door is clad in stone, and so on. Here we have an example of extraordinary design consistency for 25 projects over 25 years with no transgressions and no apparent doubts. The reductive palate of the studio abandons the conventions of skirting, cornice and architrave in favour of the more abstract. Unlike other so-called minimalists, there is an obsession in this work about the architecture of the interior, its control, its inventive detail and a particular refinement in its execution. This is exceptional.

Mark Guard is a private person and when shortlisted for the Stirling Prize back in 1997, he thought it was a moment to run for cover! With his partners, Steven and Keith, the work of their studio rarely sets off into the public realm. Conversely, their Walls and Boxes allow for the light and the character of the day to come inside, providing enhancement to those within. These works, not unlike the wagon-lit of French railways, or dare one say the interiors of very fine motor cars circa 1930, recall WH Auden's famous but ambiguous words "Private faces in public places are wiser and nicer than public faces in private places."

Edward Jones, 2016

Introduction

Mark Guard Architects began life in a kitchen in a flat in Tufnell Park, north London, in 1986. Two years later, the practice moved into a studio at the upper end of Whitfield Street in the city's West End, long before Fitzrovia's current revival. Mark Perrott Guard had spent several years working in London for Richard Rogers, Eva Jiřičná and Rick Mather. It was an inauspicious time to set up a studio. The postmodern style that began life in the 1970s left a residue of sub-standard buildings all over the city. Unbeknownst to all, the 80s boom was about to implode into the economic recession of the early 90s, characterised by a near-doubling of unemployment and a stagnation in property prices and a corresponding drop in architectural commissions. Undeterred, and with a small number of adventurous clients, the practice set about the task of re-evaluating the modern living space.

From the very earliest projects, a methodology emerged. Just as the term 'lifestyle' became ascendant in the media (and with it a swathe of media and products), the office determined that the conventional approach to living spaces was predetermined and constrictive; a house was defined by its bedrooms and reception rooms, not the overall spatial area. Instead, Guard placed an emphasis on 'transformable architecture' to redefine the domestic realm and explore ways in which a space could be practically subdivided and repurposed to accommodate a variety of uses.

Guard and his associates, Steven Pollock, Keith Tillman and Charles Barclay (who subsequently set up his own practice) built up a portfolio of residential projects, applying an approach rooted in Modernism. Guard's educational background provided the basis for a lifetime's interest in residential architecture and how it relates to the changing patterns of day-to-day life, not just the grander relationships with the wider environment.

From the very beginning of his architectural education in Canada, Mark Guard was interested in the modern house. Towards the tail-end of the first phase of Modernism, its social, aesthetic and technological factors were being supplanted by psychological ones. In particular, there was a new emphasis on the importance of physical needs over aesthetics. The University of Toronto's architecture school, under the direction of Peter Prangnell, challenged notions of architectural style and conceptual ideas in favour of a more behaviourist understanding of the interactions between people and the built environment. Analysis of small-scale elements was developed and applied to larger proposals, without the constraint of style or context.

Edward Jones, senior tutor at the Royal College of Art's School of Environmental Design in London, was a visiting tutor at the University of Toronto. The architectural

The new house in Bayswater (House 1) was constructed behind a retained facade (below). A 1:10 model was built (bottom left) to illustrate how the large window at the rear would work with the staircase enclosure and the double-height space. The team pictured in 1989, from left to right: Steven Pollock, Charles Barclay, Keith Tillman, Mark Perrott Guard.

direction at the RCA in the late 1970s under John Miller, Su Rogers and Ed Jones explored the meaning of architectural form and the relevance of building type. For contemporary architecture to have meaning, it needed to maintain a sense of historical reference and be driven by context. In contrast to the thinking at Toronto, the RCA sought contemporary architectural solutions that were typologically appropriate.

Guard was interested in these ideas and Ed Jones' ongoing re-evaluation of the pre-war Heroic period of Modernism. He transferred from the University of Toronto to the RCA in 1979 to see if his interest in Modernism could be informed by the RCA approach. These two differing approaches to finding meaning in architectural design ultimately coalesced in Guard's work into something approaching a manifesto of residential architecture comprised of two very different but equally important scales: the intimate and the contextual. Guard, together with Steven Pollock, Keith Tillman and others, has used the domestic sphere as a place to experiment quietly with these ideas.

Guard worked for the late Rick Mather from 1982 to 1985 and was influenced by Mather's early residential work (projects that were subsequently overshadowed by his later prominence as an architect of major museums). Mather created extraordinary living spaces out of unpromising contexts, making homes that were quirky, clever and adventurous, with spaces that explored the gallery, the double-height volume and the roof garden.

Pollock has worked alongside Guard since 1988. "We have our standard solutions, but what's interesting are the unusual ideas", he says, "for example the facade screen for the house in Hampstead (House 9) was initially intended to be metal and ultimately ended up as fabric." Pollock explains how materials, techniques and products are transferred from other applications. The wall copings on House 9 were made from DuPont's Corian, a material usually used in kitchens, while the fabric facade screen came from the advertising industry.

Tillman began working with Guard in 1986 whilst still studying at the University of Westminster. In 1992 Tillman began teaching part-time on a newly formed degree course in Architectural Engineering, developed at Westminster by Victoria Watson and Tillman's former teacher James Madge. Whilst there, Tillman ran his own practice and completed a number of projects before rejoining Guard in 1999. In addition to his interest in capitalising on the development of materials, Tillman acknowledges that "there is a need to retain a consistent and almost simplistic approach in the selection of bought and fabricated elements."

The new house in County Galway, Ireland (House 2, below) takes inspiration from the vernacular form of traditional stone agricultural buildings (left). These structures typically had minimal openings to the prevailing wind with livestock access on the leeward side. An external staircase provided access to a hayloft in the roof space. The cylindrical form in the new house contains the staircase.

From the outset, the practice sought to avoid unnecessary ornament. The omission of skirting boards was achieved via the use of a recessed plaster stop bead, a detail that was still quite novel in new or refurbished residential design in the early 1990s. However, the desire to remove the typical internal door proved more difficult as doors are required for privacy and for fire separation. The practice replaced the typical door and frame with a full-height pivoting door panel fitted into a recess in the wall to keep the face of the open door aligned with the wall plane. These concealed door panels allowed an open-plan living space to be subdivided into smaller spaces to suit different requirements.

Together with forward-thinking clients and the changing conditions of the London housing market, the practice developed a series of structured but flexible approaches to domestic space. The genesis of what the practice would eventually describe as 'transformable architecture' arose out of a very specific moment in London's residential development: the arrival and brief ascendancy of the loft apartment. The London loft apartment boom lagged over a decade behind the conversion fever that transformed whole swathes of New York, Chicago and other post-industrial areas from warehousing into desirable residential apartments. Lofts were originally industrial spaces adapted by artists, designers and musicians as studios and rehearsal spaces. Architectural interventions were ad hoc and functional, not necessarily built to code, and seeking mainly to make such enormous volumes of space liveable. While the original transatlantic loft living movement was initiated out of necessity and invention by working creatives, the London scene was catalysed by the early involvement of speculative developers. Industrial buildings were bought outright and carved into empty shells to be sold off and subsequently completed by the purchasers. One of London's first large scale loft developments was in Shad Thames, once the spice trading centre of London and the largest warehouse complex in the capital. The old port of London was rendered obsolete by the introduction of the shipping container, and by the early 1980s, many of its former warehouses were retained for residential conversion, including New Concordia Wharf and China Wharf. The latter were restored and converted by architects Hunt Thompson and Pollard Thomas Edwards, who reinvented the buildings as some of the capital's earliest examples of loft living.

Subsequent schemes followed in Clerkenwell and Soho. Initially, developers offered generous floorplans and genuinely spacious shells, although a paucity of design-led interiors magazines meant that inspiration was relatively thin on the ground, both for architects and purchasers.

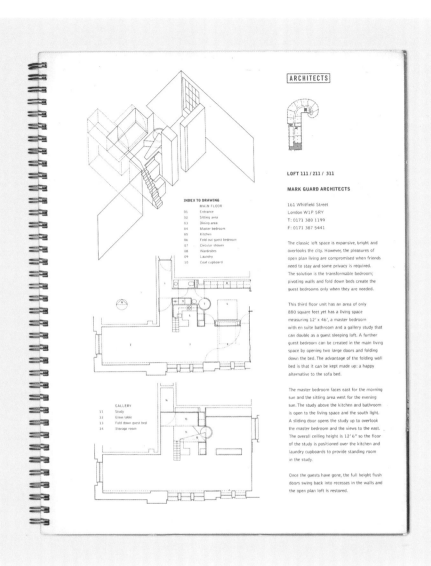

INDEX TO DRAWING

MAIN FLOOR

01	Entrance
02	Sitting area
03	Dining area
04	Master bedroom
05	Kitchen
06	Fold out guest bedroom
07	Circular shower
08	Wardrobes
09	Laundry
10	Coat cupboard

GALLERY

11	Study
12	Glass table
13	Fold down guest bed
14	Storage room

LOFT 111 / 211 / 311

MARK GUARD ARCHITECTS

161 Whitfield Street
London W1P 5RY
T: 0171 380 1199
F: 0171 387 5441

The classic loft space is expansive, bright and
overlooks the city. However, the pleasures of
open plan living are compromised when friends
need to stay and some privacy is required.
The solution is the transformable bedroom;
pivoting walls and fold down beds create the
guest bedrooms only when they are needed.

This third floor unit has an area of only
880 square feet yet has a living space
measuring 12' x 46', a master bedroom
with en suite bathroom and a gallery study that
can double as a guest sleeping loft. A further
guest bedroom can be created in the main living
space by opening two large doors and folding
down the bed. The advantage of the folding wall
bed is that it can be kept made up: a happy
alternative to the sofa bed.

The master bedroom faces east for the morning
sun and the sitting area west for the evening
sun. The study above the kitchen and bathroom
is open to the living space and the south light.
A sliding door opens the study up to overlook
the master bedroom and the views to the east.
The overall ceiling height is 12' 6" so the floor
of the study is positioned over the kitchen and
laundry cupboards to provide standing room
in the study.

Once the guests have gone, the full height flush
doors swing back into recesses in the walls and
the open plan loft is restored.

The brochure for
the Manhattan Loft
Corporation's Bankside
Lofts development, 1997,
included a speculative
scheme by Mark Guard
Architects for one of
the units. The brochure
included a number of
proposals by different
architects to illustrate the
ways in which the shell
units could be fitted out.
Mark Guard Architects'
design for this particular
unit was adopted and
revised, resulting in
Loft 4 (page 62).

In 1992 the Manhattan Loft Corporation was established. Founded by the American developer Harry Handelsman, the MLC pioneered American-style loft living in London. Boldly marketed, with strong graphics and a tough, quasi-industrial aesthetic, the MLC began with the Summer Street Lofts in Clerkenwell and the Soho Lofts in Wardour Street, reconfigured by CZWG, launched in 1993. As part of the marketing materials for the latter, several contemporary architects were invited to draw up speculative schemes to showcase how these empty, unprepossessing spaces could be made habitable.

Mark Guard Architects' speculative scheme led to a number of commissions, in both Soho and Bankside Lofts. At the core of the original proposal was the idea of transformability, a space that could be constantly changed and adapted, not only to maximise the available floorplan but to create a point of focus during the domestic routine, as well as exploiting natural light and views wherever possible. "Once the guests have gone, the full-height flush doors swing back into recesses in the walls and the open-plan loft is restored", the brochure read. Such ideas had been evident in the studio's earliest residential work, including the conversion of a small mansion block apartment in Kensington (Apartment 1), where a typical small apartment became an ever-changing series of rooms, separated by large pivoting doors that could be rearranged to change the emphasis on the space.

Mark Guard Architects (the practice became Guard Tillman Pollock in 2002) was one of the first London architecture firms to work on lofts, but it was practically unique in its approach to these often awkward and idiosyncratic spaces. In reshaping empty interiors, the practice carved architectonic spaces out of empty shells, creating internal landscapes. Guard, Tillman and Pollock are interested in both the appropriateness of a design as well as the functional liveability of a layout. They like simple spaces, layered with function, demonstrating an uncompromised clarity of detail design and high levels of technical knowledge. Their approach is paired with the emphasis on objects such as columns, staircases or fireplaces that engender a relationship between place and person. These interiors, with their functional components separated into discrete cubes, cylinders and walls, act as a surrogate for the lack of outdoor spaces. At the same time, the floorplan emphasises a multiplicity of routes, helping to change the perception of the space.

The multifunctional wall was an element developed for the first Manhattan Loft concept flat, and subsequently found its way into several projects. Guard describes walls as connective devices and interiors as landscapes.

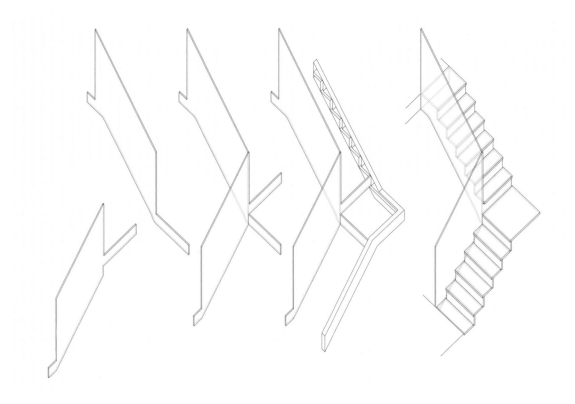

The glass staircase in Apartment 7 uses concealed metal clamps and strings to preserve the appearance of an all-glass staircase with no visible fixings or mastics. As a result, the glass steps and landing cantilever directly out from an unbroken wall plane. The balustrades float free of the treads and are formed from two pieces of laminated glass set at 90 degrees to each other, held in place by hidden clamps. All glass edges remain visible.

Rather than a wall that just acts as a container of space, a wall as a free-standing object in an interior can order the layout, emphasise dimension and link different elements together. At the Shad Thames apartment (Loft 6), the expansive post-industrial space is bisected by a single wall, a grand connective gesture that unites an otherwise featureless landscape, directing the eye towards the river views while concealing the guest bedroom, bathroom, kitchen and utility space. In the Holland Park apartment (Apartment 6), a black basalt storage wall orders the plan and creates the long vista.

Guard Tillman Pollock's constant search for simplification places the emphasis on space and light rather than ornament. By 'floating' walls above a recessed plaster bead instead of skirtings, and by combining these with floor-to-ceiling mullionless windows wherever possible, or a rooflight above, the projects serve as contemplative and light-filled backdrops for the occupant's possessions and home life. The concealed door is a key component of these projects, allowing internal spaces to flow into one another without the hindrance of the door frame. Further simplification is achieved by the concealment of the radiator (or its replacement with underfloor heating), the disguising of the light switch and the omission of the door handle.

The frameless glass floor and staircase was another development. The glass stair became an iconic design statement in the 1980s, with architects—most notably Eva Jiřičná—producing beautifully detailed, intricate, structural designs. In contrast, Guard Tillman Pollock's staircases were constructed with limited budgets and were made from laminated glass treads supported by plywood concealed behind the plasterboard. A similar system was used for clear span glass balustrades, avoiding the visual distraction of rails, fixings or mastic. In House 3, Orla Kelly designed the glass balustrade beneath a glass shelf, supported by a second clear span glass leg, elegantly resolving the lateral load problem without the need for other supports (page 23). In Apartment 7, Tillman resolved the detail of a glass balustrade adjoining a glass stair by cantilevering the glass steps from a steel string concealed behind the wall. The balustrades overlap each other and are individually clamped into the strings, allowing them to float free of the end of the glass steps. The finished stair has no visible mastic and all glass edges remain visible. It is not just the attention to detail but it is the inventive detail that makes these projects special.

As the London apartment market matured through the late 90s onwards, shells became more and more uncommon. Overseas investment buying and speculation became in many respects an enemy of good design, as market expectations

The connection between the new house in Hampstead (House 9) and the adjoining Victorian terrace is modulated by a number of visual elements. These soften the transition and help integrate the new house into the streetscape. Images of the house before and after the installation of the mesh screen show how the stretched fabric completes the floating box and encloses the private balcony gardens behind.

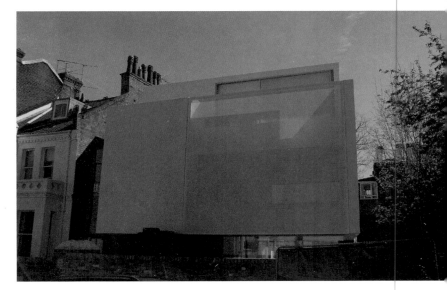

overrode innovation and individuality. The practice shifted focus to new-build residential and radical reconstructions, allowing for further exploration. Yet rather than simply use the formal language of high Modernism, the practice's evolving vocabulary explored pragmatic methods for enhancing life at high density, when space, light and privacy were at an ever-increasing premium. These affirmative transformations are the opposite of the monastic, arid and lifeless image of Minimalism.

The desire to maximise light and space and to simplify visual detail to make less prescriptive spaces is complemented by the incorporation of built objects such as free-standing walls, boxes or cylinders. These objects, together with purpose-designed elements—the fireplace, the bath—combined with the ability to change and adjust the space, engender a relationship between the occupier and the architecture. At a different scale, the practice's new-build houses demonstrate

a concern with the relationship to their neighbours and seek to find an appropriateness and meaning through building type. In an era where whim and gratuitous gesture has taken prominence, the practice relies on the tradition of a disciplined and rigorous approach to building design. The combination of the small scale and the tactile with the larger issue of context and meaning has provided Guard, Tillman and Pollock with a controlled but rich language to reconsider the Heroic period of modern architecture.

From the landscape of the home to the landscape of the city, the practice highlights the relationship between human scale and the world at large. This approach might appear superficially niche, but the overarching themes are increasingly pertinent. In the UK it is predicted that by 2033 some 41 per cent of all households will consist of only one person. Not only are one- and two-person households on the rise, but rising house prices and land

values favour a tiny, privileged percentage of the population. The blank canvases of the loft boom are all filled, and while in London, and many other cities, apartment living is back on the agenda, it is driven by private investment with little motivation to enhance wider social capital. Architecture designed to accommodate changing demands is hardly new but has never been more relevant.

Most architectural studios look to grow in size and seek ever more ambitious projects. Guard, Tillman and Pollock have chosen to improve their understanding of architecture through a succession of residential projects where they can discover new solutions to old problems. As fashion changes, they continue to promote the utopian modernist vision of maximising space with function and flexibility. They believe that architecture can do more than simply resolve the brief—it must also enhance the spirit.

Jonathan Bell, 2016

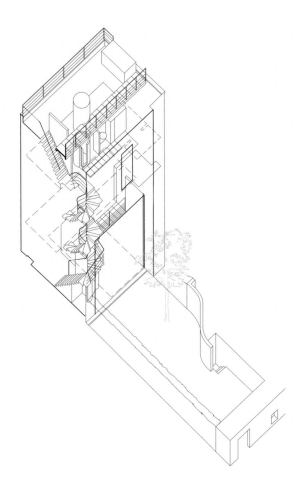

Bayswater, London
Guard / Barclay, 1990

This four-storey, four-bedroom house is set behind a retained and extended traditional front facade on a private garden square in west London. A contemporary facade at the rear overlooks a public road. Together with the gravel garden, the strong geometry evokes memories of the heroic domestic architecture of the early Modern movement. The unusual layout includes a 'flying freehold' above the entrance hall to the adjoining property. The shallow floorplan comprises of a front-to-back dining room on the ground floor, a double-cube vertical void space at the rear and a double-cube sitting room that spans the full width of the house—a *piano nobile*. The open-plan interior is achieved using full-height doors recessed into wall pockets. These are held open by electromagnets that allow the doors to close automatically when activated by the smoke detection system or if closed by a switch. With concrete floors, metal staircase and white plaster walls, the house has a deliberately robust aesthetic.

New-build four-storey terrace house behind retained front facade. Steel frame with timber floor structure and concrete block walls. Polished concrete ground floor, maple wood to upper floors. Shot-blasted and lacquered folded steel plate staircase. Smooth plaster to walls and ceilings. Full-height sliding and pivoting doors. Stainless steel kitchen. Smooth render to exterior walls. Gravelled garden. 180m²

House 1

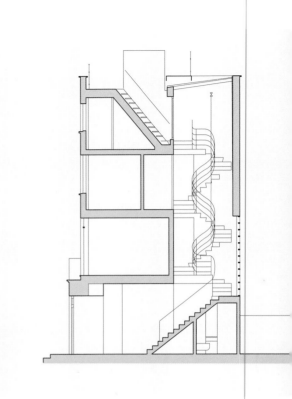

The Suspended Stair

The folded sheet steel
staircase is suspended
from a thin steel rod,
reducing the visual space
it occupies. The typical
stair string is omitted and
the folded underside of the
steel steps are expressed.
The staircase is set away
from the walls, creating
shadows and silhouettes
on the walls and floor
below, while the shot-
blasted and lacquered
metallic finish reflects
light from the large window
and rooflight above.

Before

After

The Glazed Screen

The large window at
the back of the house is
overlooked by properties
on the other side of the
road. The strong horizontal
glazing bars create a form
of screening, giving the
interior a sense of privacy
without compromising
the light and views of the
garden and trees.

Kensington, London
Guard / Tillman, 1991

With a large roof terrace to the east and another to the west, the layout of this one-bedroom mansion block apartment needed radical rethinking to maximise the potential for space, light and views. By moving the front door, it was possible to adapt the European *enfilade* planning approach and link all the main rooms along a central axis to connect the roof terraces at either end, exploiting the long views and natural light. Floor-to-ceiling sliding and folding doors allow flexibility of space and use. The apartment can either be open plan, or if some or all of the doors are closed it can be reconfigured to create a number of different internal layouts to suit different requirements throughout the day.

Reconfigured third-floor apartment in 1920s mansion block. Carpeted raised timber floor. Smooth plaster to walls and ceilings. Full-height sliding and pivoting doors with concealed handles. Floor-to-ceiling blinds. 68m²

Apartment 1

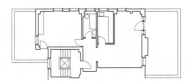

Before

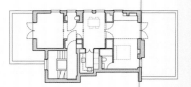

After

Configurations:
01 Open plan
02 Bedroom
03 Dressing
04 Quiet study
05 Business meeting
06 Unwanted caller
07 Evening guest
08 Caller during supper
09 Guest suite
10 Guest breakfast
11 Closed plan

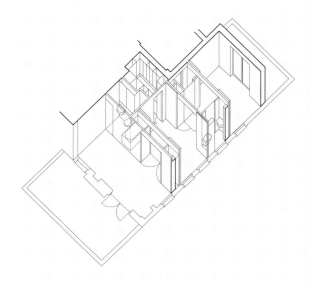

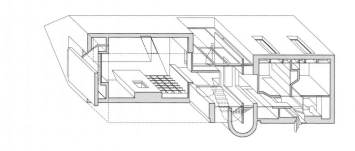

Galway, Ireland
Guard / Pollock, 1992

Set amongst a landscape of rural development, this new house in County Galway draws inspiration from traditional Irish vernacular buildings but with some modernist influence. The curved top-lit staircase signifies the entrance and window positions seek to conceal the internal layout. The children's bedrooms are on the ground floor with direct access to a basement playroom and to the garden. A south-facing double-height entrance hall links the ground-floor kitchen/dining space to the first-floor sitting room, which is arranged to overlook Lough Corrib, the largest of the Connemara lakes. A small terrace with a traditional external staircase links the raised sitting room to the garden.

New-build two-storey detached house with attic room and part basement. Concrete frame and concrete block. Maple wood floors. Smooth plaster to walls and ceilings. Full-height sliding and pivoting doors. Smooth render to exterior walls. Gravel driveway. 195m²

House 2

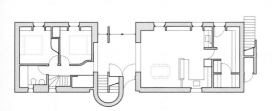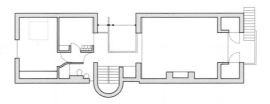

The Vernacular Form

The house references rural Irish vernacular architecture without being explicit, taking elements from traditional barn design with modest proportions and scale. The elevations deliberately disguise the floor arrangement, while the small windows and external gable staircase evoke simple agricultural structures.

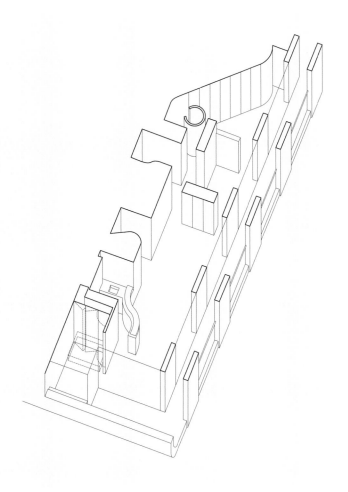

Barbican, London
Guard / Tillman, 1992

This apartment on the thirty-sixth floor of one of the three towers in London's Barbican complex had an existing typical internal layout with a dark corridor and small bedrooms that failed to do justice to the extraordinary views over north and west London. Removing the internal partitions allowed the full length of the apartment to be revealed, broken only by a number of sculptural elements including the curved glass kitchen counter and the study box. Through the arrangement of concealed full-height folding doors the master bedroom suite can be expanded to include the study and the second bathroom when needed. The open floorplan helps to create an ethereal world that is in keeping with the huge views.

Reconfigured tower block apartment. Carpet to existing floor. Smooth plaster to walls and ceiling. Full-height sliding and pivoting doors. Stainless steel kitchen. 105m²

Apartment 2

Before

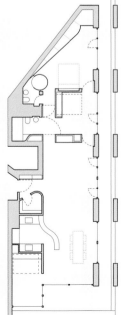

After

The Internal Landscape

This long vista contains a
study 'box' and bespoke
cabinetry housing the
television and storage.
Full-height doors separate
this space from the living
room and bedroom, or can
be folded back to preserve
the long vista. The circular
shower drum is constructed
from glass blocks and adds
reflections to the white-
walled and carpeted space.

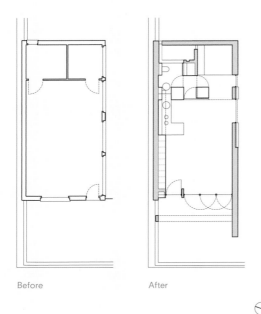

Before   After

Apartment 3

Fifth Arrondissement, Paris
Guard / Tillman, 1994

Approached by a long walk over the roofscape, this former one-room caretaker's apartment sits on top of an eight-storey 1930s apartment building in Paris' Fifth Arrondissement. Within the 34 square-metre footprint, the space was reconfigured to create a separate bedroom with a number of different internal arrangements, achieved by sliding or swinging various internal floor-to-ceiling doors. The apartment can be opened up to maintain the full visual dimensions of the space or closed down as required. Three boxes contain the components of the kitchen, bathroom and storage space. The bathroom washbasin forms part of the kitchen worktop, separated by electronic glass that provides privacy when needed. A portal frame and glass canopy frame extraordinary views of the Paris skyline.

Reconstructed rooftop penthouse. Limestone floor. Smooth plaster to walls and ceiling. Full-height sliding and pivoting doors. Stone bath. Stainless steel kitchen. Smooth render to external walls. Limestone terrace. 34m²

The Sliding Wall

In small spaces the sight of the maximum dimension can reduce the feeling of claustrophobia. Sliding the wall to close off the bedroom reveals the route to the bathroom and an alternative route to the bedroom. A pivoting door behind the sliding wall creates an en-suite arrangement for the bedroom and a lobby for the bathroom.

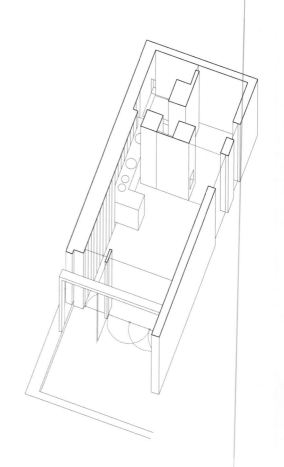

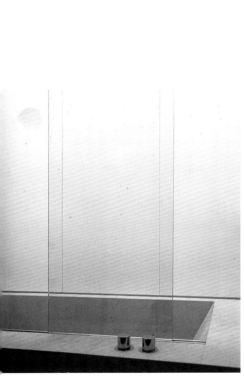

Queen's Park, London
Guard / Pollock, 1993

The problem with the ubiquitous two-storey London Victorian terrace house is that the rear extension cuts off the main reception rooms from the rear garden. In this house the plan is turned upside down. The kitchen and living space are moved to an open-plan first floor and the bedrooms placed in the darker ground floor. Rooflights and glass floors bring light into the heart of the house, while a double-height glazed rear facade integrates both floors with the garden. The floor changes level to suit the use of the long stainless steel counter, as it changes from coffee table to worktop to breakfast table.

Reconfigured Victorian terrace house. Pine flooring. Smooth plaster to walls and ceilings. Stainless steel linear kitchen. Frameless glass balustrade. Double-height space to opening rear glazed screen. Timber decking. 128m²

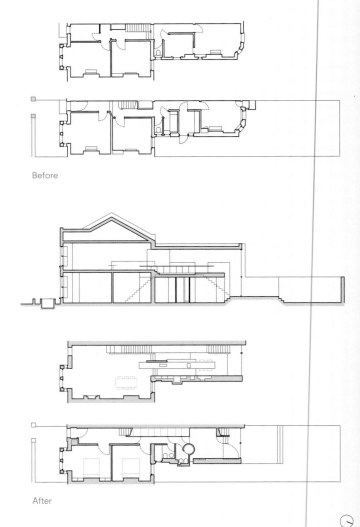

Before

After

House 3

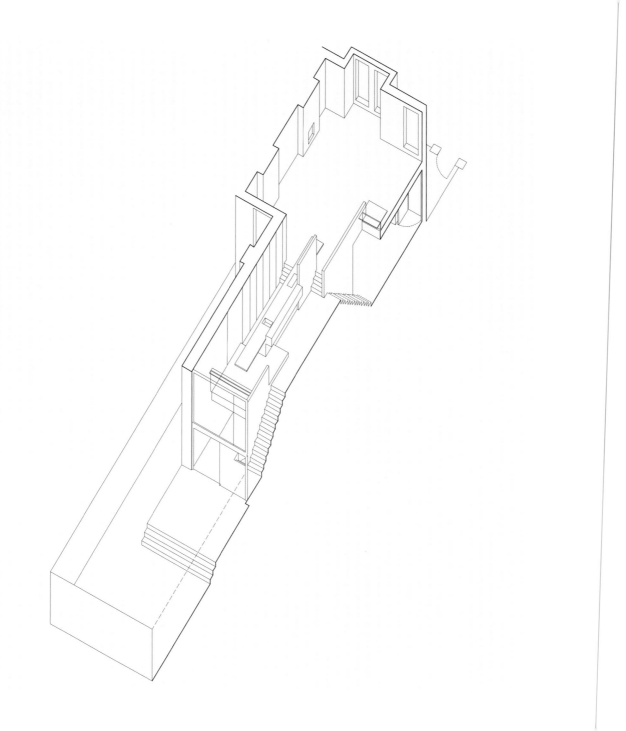

The Second Stair

The addition of a second staircase creates numerous permutations for routes around the house, as well as making a direct connection between the first-floor reception rooms and the rear garden, avoiding the need to always pass through the entrance hall.

Fitzrovia, London
Guard / Pollock, 1994

The top two floors of this typical Georgian London house had been converted into a living room and separate kitchen on the lower floor and two bedrooms and a bathroom on the upper floor. The reconfigured space creates an open-plan kitchen, dining and living space on the top floor, with access to a roof terrace and two transformable bedrooms, a shower room and a study on the lower floor. A full-width single sheet skylight brings sunlight into the kitchen/dining area and a glass table and glass floor channel natural light to the floor below. The rear balcony is arranged for ventilation rather than views, bringing fresh air and city sounds to the dining table under the glass roof.

Reconfigured maisonette in Georgian town house. Maple flooring. Smooth plaster to walls and ceilings. Stainless steel kitchen. Glass staircase. Frameless clear span glass rooflight. Circular shower and transformable bedrooms. 86m²

Apartment 4

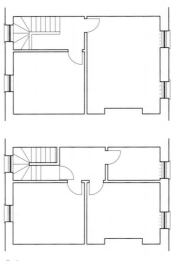

Before

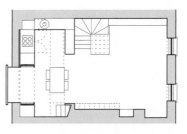

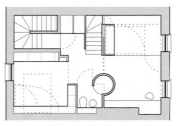

After

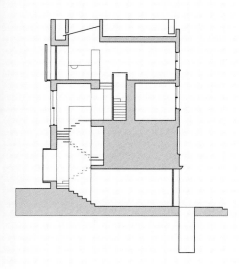

The Sense of Outside

The single sheet double-glazed rooflight (the largest possible at the time of installation) spans the entire width of the house. By concealing all the frames within the walls and by carrying those walls up above the glass, the perception of the glass plane is diluted. The sounds of the city filter through the 'viewless' balcony, adding to the effect.

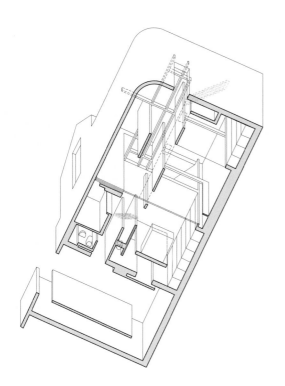

Deptford, London,
Guard / Pollock, 1995

This Victorian brick coach house had been extended on both sides with rudimentary roofing and used as a car repair workshop. By removing these metal roofs the site was transformed into a two-bedroom house with an entrance courtyard to one side and a private walled garden to the other. The living room and kitchen are placed on the first floor, with bedrooms on the ground floor. The east wall of the former coach house is replaced with glass panels that slide on the outside of the facade, opening up the interior of the house to the walled garden. Steel beams brace the brick garden walls and provide support for the free-standing walls and the sliding glass panels. With the glass panels slid to one side, the walled garden becomes an extension of the house. The high garden walls create a secure private world so that the house can open onto the walled garden on balmy summer nights.

Reconstructed car repair workshop incorporating Victorian coach house. Brick walls and slate roof. Concrete ground floors, bedhead and free-standing garden walls. Smooth plaster to walls and ceilings. Timber first floor. Exposed exterior steel frame to brace existing brick garden walls. Sliding glass panels. Gravel courtyard. 90m²

House 4

The Open Facade

The house is planned so that the glass panels to the living room, bedroom and garden study can be slid to one side so the whole facade can be opened up to the walled courtyard garden. In the main house the three glass panels on each floor slide towards the road to sit in front of the solid wall to the second bedroom and kitchen above. To open up the garden studio/study, the two glass panels can be slid across the courtyard to sit in the garden next to the boundary wall.

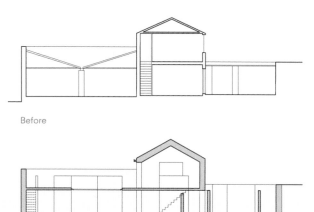

Before

After

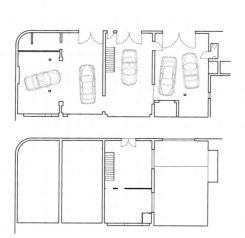

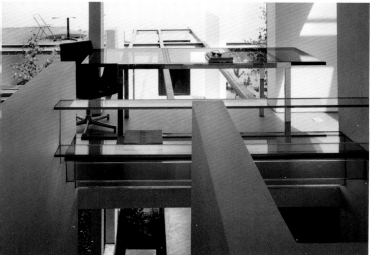

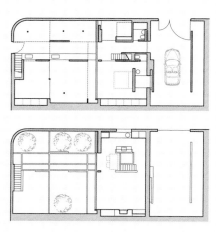

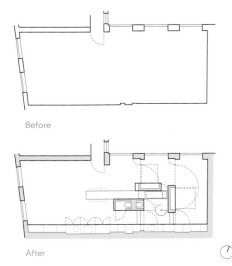

Before

After

Soho, London
Guard / Pollock, 1996

Given an empty rectangular loft space in London's West End, the challenge was to see if three boxes, a table and a circular glass shower placed in the centre of the floorplan could be used to make a transformable, open-plan space into a two-bedroom apartment with bathroom and cloakroom. Large pivoting doors on two of the boxes swing open to create walls, allowing beds to be pulled down in each bedroom. Full-height doors create the bathroom, the bath being formed out of part of the stainless steel dining table, with an electric glass screen providing privacy. The long storage wall contains the kitchen, utility area, hi-fi and wardrobes. The space can be easily changed each day from an open-plan space to a one- or two-bedroom apartment, depending on the need of the occupier. The transformable arrangement offers the ultimate practicality in the inner city.

Shell loft space in former industrial building. Limestone flooring. Smooth plaster to walls and ceiling. Stainless steel kitchen. Stainless steel dining table incorporating bath. Circular glass shower. Full-height doors. Fold-down beds. Electric privacy glass. 90m²

Loft 1

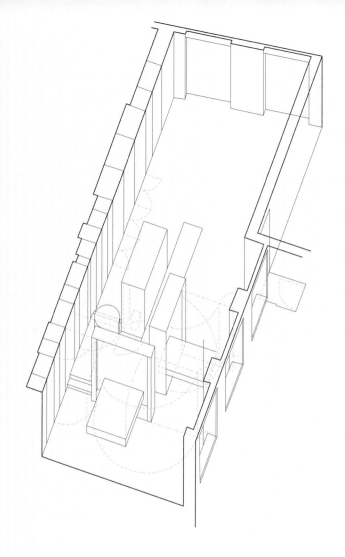

The Free-Standing Box

Rooms are formed by
pivoting doors that fold out
from free-standing boxes,
creating private bedrooms.
Rather than containing
space as a wall might do,
the box is contained within
a larger space, increasing
the perception of the size
of the apartment while
contributing to the storage
space and providing
places to conceal the
beds. The home becomes
a transformable internal
landscape rather than a
series of different rooms.

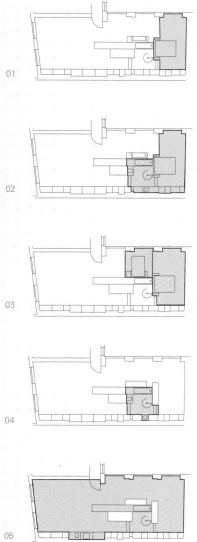

01

02

03

04

05

Configurations:
01 Master bedroom
02 En-suite bathroom
03 Two bedrooms
04 Bathroom
05 Open plan

Soho, London
Guard / Pollock, 1996

Placing the bathroom and kitchen in a series of aligned walls in this small central London loft permitted an en-suite arrangement for the bedroom and maximum space for the living area. The box next to the kitchen contains the bath and shower. Both sections of the bathroom can be closed off with individual doors. The remainder of the bath box contains a utility area and kitchen appliances. A lowered ceiling strip is suspended to provide task lighting for the kitchen and uplighting to the main space. The linear arrangement of the bathroom and kitchen maximises the living space and emphasises the length of the apartment, creating a space that appears far larger than it is.

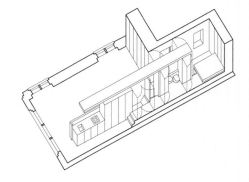

Loft. Maple timber floors. Smooth plaster to walls and ceilings. Exposed painted brickwork. Full-height pivoting doors. Stainless steel bath and kitchen. 64m²

Loft 2

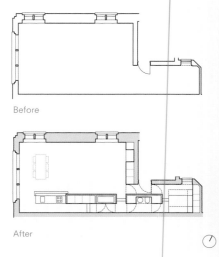

Before

After

The Hidden Kitchen

In small open-plan
spaces there is a danger
of ending up living in a
kitchen. To avoid this
problem, the recognisable
elements of a kitchen—
the oven, extract hood,
over-counter cupboard
and work surfaces—need
to be concealed from
view. In this project a
raised wall hides the
worktop and the storage
and appliances are placed
under the counter and
in the adjoining box.
Without compromising
the function, the kitchen
is reduced to a plastered
wall silhouetted in front
of a painted brick wall.

Queen's Park, London
Guard / Hutchinson, 1998

This studio for a photographer transformed an awkward loft space created out of a former industrial building in west London. The layout takes full advantage of an existing mezzanine, incorporating a bathroom beneath the roof slope and providing storage in a free-standing box for clothes and a fold-down master bed. A second shower room on the lower level serves the second bedroom, which also doubles up as a changing space for models.

Loft fit-out. White industrial flooring. White walls. Floor-to-ceiling pivoting doors. Plywood staircase and gallery flooring. 133m²

Loft 3

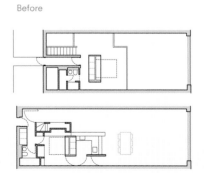

Before

After

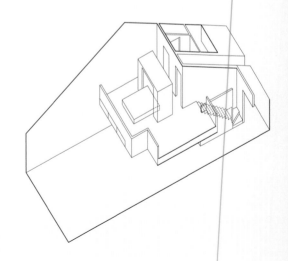

The Live/Work Space

This live/work space
needed to operate as
a photographic studio
during the day and
transform into the client's
home in the evenings.
A further requirement
was for the storage
of rolls of material,
some up to 4 metres
long, for photographic
backdrops. To keep
the sense of space,
the existing wall planes
needed to remain, so
the raised gallery floor
has linear storage
compartments within
the floor thickness,
accessed from the
double-height space.

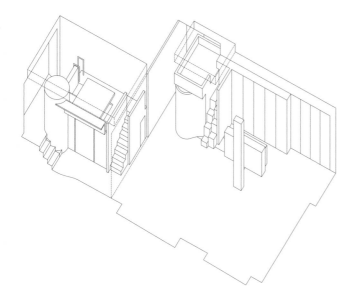

Southbank, London
Guard / Pollock, 1998

This loft in a former industrial building in south London had a 3.4 metre-high ceiling, not enough height for two storeys. By utilising the wasted space beneath the beds, sufficient height was found for two galleried bedrooms. With an uninspiring outlook and no rooflighting, the interior needed objects that could be silhouetted against the available natural light: an internal landscape. The form of the cylindrical guest shower/cloakroom is repeated in a circular WC room. The guest sleeping platform is located above the cloakroom and the master bedroom is above the dressing room. A 4 × 3.1 metre-high sliding wall separates the master bedroom from the living space when privacy is required and doubles as a film projection screen. The kitchen has a wash-up area in the cupboards and cooking area on the island, with glass shelves acting as plate warmers.

Loft fit-out. Limestone floors. Smooth plaster to walls and ceilings. Exposed concrete column. Large sliding partition. Raised gallery bedrooms. Stone bath. Stainless steel kitchen counters and hand washbasins. 91m²

Loft 4

The Home Movie

The 4 × 3.1 metre-high sliding wall that separates the master bedroom from the living space was constructed from stretched canvas to reduce the rolling weight and maintain a smooth, seamless surface. By placing a concealed projector in the lowered ceiling above the living space, the wall becomes the screen, transforming the apartment into a private cinema.

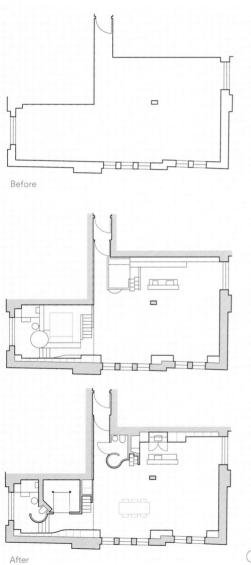

Before

After

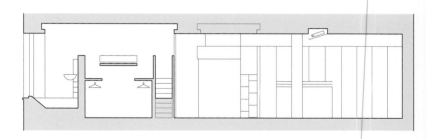

The Gallery Bedroom

The master bedroom is above the walk-in dressing room. By reducing the height of the hanging spaces a lowered floor is formed on both sides and at the end of the bed creating a normal bedroom with bed access on all sides. Although not used on a regular basis, a purpose-made swimming pool ladder provides an alternative route to the master bathroom.

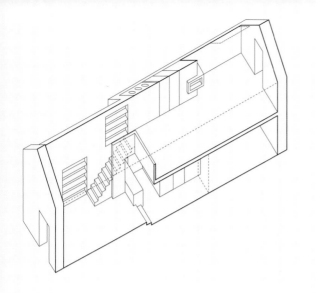

County Kilkenny, Ireland
Guard / Hutchinson, 1999

This former traditional stone barn sits alongside a narrow rural lane. Over the years, the growing size of farm machinery had resulted in part of the rear wall of the building being demolished to increase the width of the road, giving the interior of the building an odd and uncomfortable shape. The conversion rationalises the interior proportions through the insertion of a new white wall that runs the length of the lane boundary. The wall creates a conventional rectangular living space, positions the staircase up to the galleried living area and terminates at a cantilevered fireplace. Light tubes contained within the wall direct natural light to the kitchen and bathroom below. New galvanised metal rooflights flood the space with natural light.

Former agricultural building. Restored exposed stone walls. Smooth plaster to walls and ceilings. Painted timber trusses. Galvanised metal rooflights. Timber tilt and turn doors and windows. Stained pine floors. 71m²

House 5

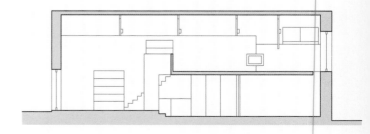

The Old and The New

The new linear white storage wall interlinks the different levels of the original building and creates an increased sense of space. The original roof trusses are retained and painted white. The rough and the smooth complement each other to create a rich interior that acknowledges the age and history of the building.

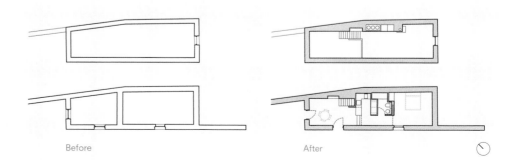

Before

After

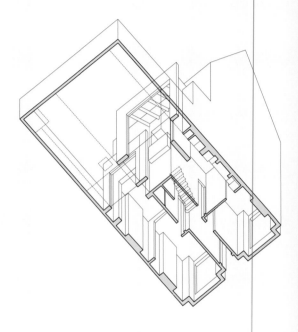

House 6

Refurbished Edwardian terrace house. Limestone floors to kitchen and new extension. Smooth plaster to walls and ceilings. Motorised sliding glass doors. Frameless glazed roof. White rendered walls to garden enclosing pond and limestone paving. 200m²

Chiswick, London
Guard / Pollock, 2000

This Edwardian terrace house is located on the Bedford Estate, one of London's garden city suburbs. An elegant double-fronted facade to the tree-lined street was not reflected at the rear, where a brick-built utility room and cloakroom cut off the connection to the garden. The solution was to restructure the rear of the property, replacing the original brick with a combination of structural glass and white rendered elements, setting up a series of frames to create new vistas through the house. The new addition creates a second route from the kitchen/breakfast room to the sitting room, with a long vista through the living room across the new pond. The new additions were arranged as a series of portal frames braced by structural glass beams that also support the structural glass roof of the new rear addition. Motorised glass doors slide into pockets in the free-standing walls, opening up the internal space to the walled garden and pond.

The Layered Facade

The glass conservatory is a useful addition to many houses. However, it is less successful if it increases overlooking or solar gain. Here, masonry walls are arranged to create a layered rear facade, modulating the transition from inside to outside. The walls permit the glass doors to slide away into pockets, avoiding the busy visual effect of stacked pieces of glass. When the sliding doors are concealed within the free-standing walls, the extension becomes part of the walled garden.

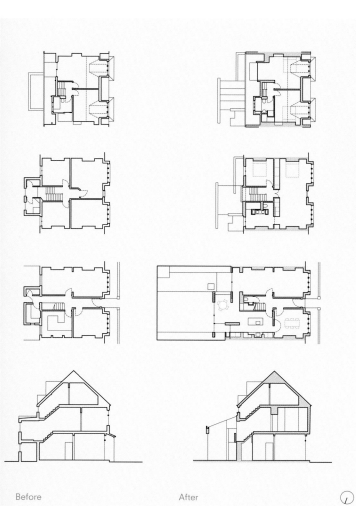

Before   After   ①

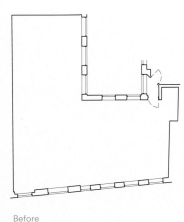
Before

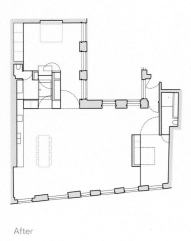
After

Soho, London
Tillman, 2003

This loft space had a single facade with views to the street; all other windows face onto an overlooked light well. To create a large flexible living space, the master bedroom needed to be placed alongside the light well. The bathroom is placed in the centre of the space and is arranged to maintain views from the bedroom over the large stone bath to the street beyond. Above the bath are moveable screens to create privacy when required. A linear kitchen responds to the strong horizontal forms of the existing ceiling beams, while a separate transformable study/ guest bedroom can be made en suite to the cloakroom/shower room or be turned into a free-standing box.

Loft fit-out. Maple flooring. White plaster to walls and ceilings. White painted exposed steel beams. Grey limestone bedhead and bath. Stainless steel kitchen and washbasin. 170m²

Loft 5

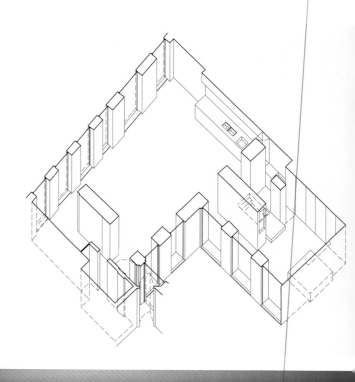

The Private Public Space

The challenge is to create an open-plan space with a degree of flexible privacy. In this apartment, transformable moveable walls open up vistas that create views right into the deep plan, allowing occupiers of the master bedroom to look across and through the bathroom area to the street facade when desirable.

Tower Bridge, London
Guard / Barclay, 1996
Tillman / Mais, 2004

The former Victorian warehouse on the south side of the River Thames was one of the first industrial buildings to be divided up and sold as residential shells. Dark, oddly-shaped but with stunning views of the river and the City, the space needed a strong intervention. This was achieved with a 23-metre wall, the longest possible dimension, to divide the living space from the services and bedrooms. The master bedroom and bathroom are next to the river, arranged to afford views of Tower Bridge. The master bedroom can be closed off or made into an extension of the living space. A large sliding panel with built-in rotating television can be slid across to hide the bedroom and expose a large projection screen. The dining table and the kitchen table are on tracks recessed into the stone floor so that they can be easily slid to different positions for different occasions, including the terrace in good weather.

Loft fit-out. Limestone floor. White plaster to walls and ceilings. Floating black basalt wall. Glass and stainless steel sliding dining table and stainless steel kitchen. 197m²

Loft 6

The Maximum Dimension

A way to increase the
apparent size of any
space is to exploit the
longest available internal
dimension and create
a sense of enhanced
perspective. In this
apartment, the largest
dimension bisects the
irregularly shaped space
and is defined by a wall
that separates the service
elements from the public
elements. Openings
punctuate the wall,
behind which are
concealed bathrooms,
study/bedroom, kitchen
and utility area.

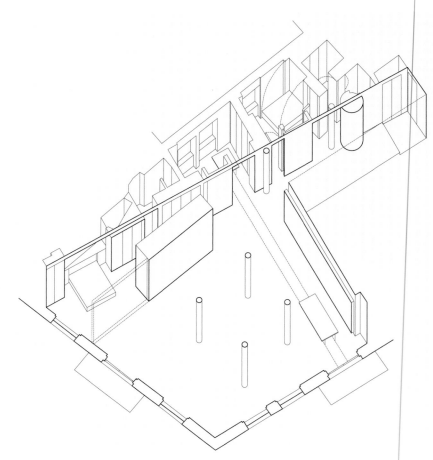

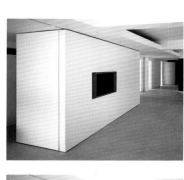

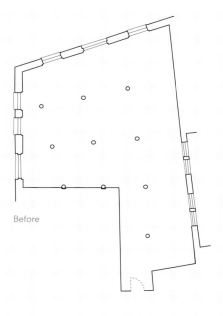

Before

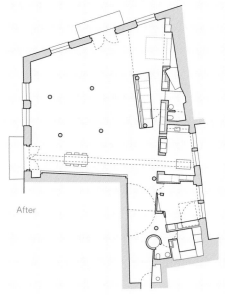

After

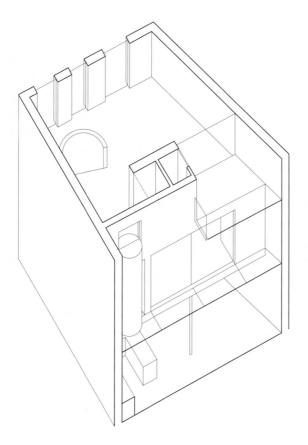

Kensington, London
Tillman, 2005

The London mews house, originally designed for the horse, carriage and driver, typically has no garden or windows at the rear. This mews house in Kensington was unusual in having a slim rear light well to serve the upper floors. To provide more natural light to the ground-floor living space, this light well was extended to the full width of the property and a glass floor installed at first-floor level to light the rear wall plane. The result is a dramatic backdrop to the main ground-floor living space. The overlooked windows to the master bedroom were removed and replaced with full-width, floor-to-ceiling glazing opening on to the light well. On the top floor, the light well was expanded to create a sunny external terrace connected to the sitting room.

Refurbished mews house. Limestone flooring. Smooth plaster to walls and ceilings. Painted steel columns. Frameless glass terraces. 180m²

House 7

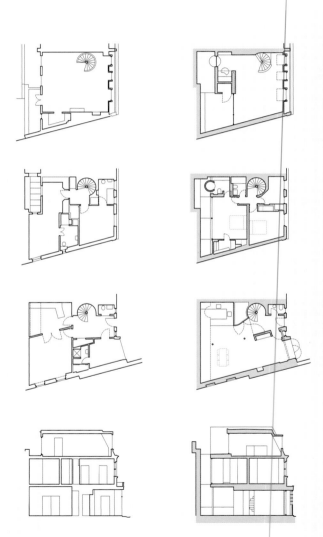

Before

After

The Glass Slot

The use of glass to expand the visual dimensions of a space is a key device. Minimal or frameless glazing details result in rooflights, floors, bridges, slots and balustrades that provide seamless links with rooms, floors, exteriors and interiors. Large pieces of frameless glass can fool the eye and appear to make the material disappear, providing an extraordinary connection between the sky and the interior.

Apartment 5

Kensington, London
Guard / Du Toit, 2007

This apartment in a post-war apartment block in Kensington was designed to exploit the rare configuration: a 27 metre-long lateral space that overlooks a garden square. The rearranged apartment takes maximum advantage of the long dimension, with a series of full-height sliding doors that can be opened up to present a long, unbroken vista running the length of the space. The mansard slope to the front of the apartment is concealed behind a run of vertical walls and concealed cupboards. The new living spaces are defined by a series of boxes constructed from dark stained wood, containing kitchen equipment, coat cupboards and study, which are offset strongly by the white perimeter walls. The loose arrangement of these boxes creates different routes within the apartment, adding to the increased perception of the space.

Reconfigured post-war apartment. Stained oak flooring. White plaster to walls and ceilings. Black stained timber storage boxes. Black stained timber kitchen. Grey limestone fireplace, window thresholds, washbasins and bath. Full-height sliding and pivoting doors. 166m²

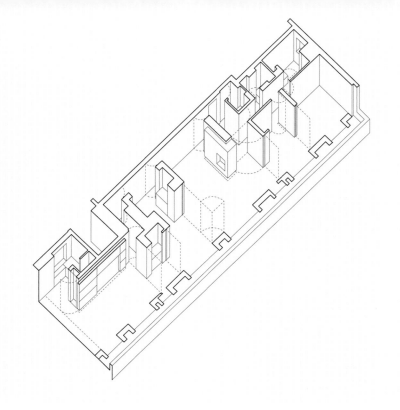

The Invisible Door

Flat, full-height doors fitted in a wall recess can be made to appear as a continuation of the wall plane and form the essential building blocks of transformable space. These concealed doors pivot or slide to change an open-plan space into a multi-bedroom apartment.

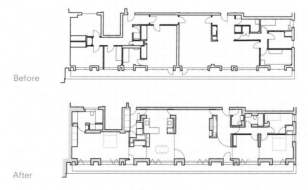

Before

After

Refurbished semi-detached house. Polished concrete floor. Stained oak upper floors. Smooth plaster to walls and ceilings. Full-height flush doors and restored period features. Frameless glass balustrade. Stainless steel kitchen. 270m²

Islington, London
Guard / Tillman, 2009

The traditional Victorian London terrace house was arranged with the kitchen in the basement, accessed by a reversed narrow stair and cut off from the main living accommodation on the raised ground floor. To connect the basement kitchen and dining room with the ground-floor reception room, the existing main staircase is extended down to basement level and a double-height void space created at the rear. A frameless pivoting glass window creates views from the reception room to the Tom Stuart-Smith-designed garden, as well as bringing natural light into the kitchen and dining room below. The new window allows the house to be opened up to the garden and the living space extended in the summer months.

House 8

The Audible Connection

The rearrangement of the interior volume and the rearranged staircase not only makes a new visual and spatial connection between the reception rooms but an audible one, bringing a social dimension to the space as well as the outdoor sounds of the garden into the sitting room at ground-floor level.

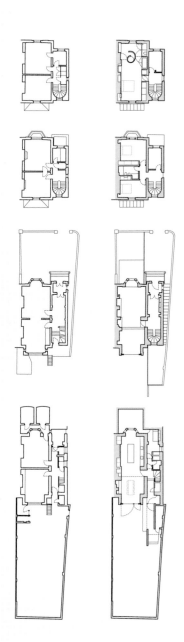

Before   After   ⊖

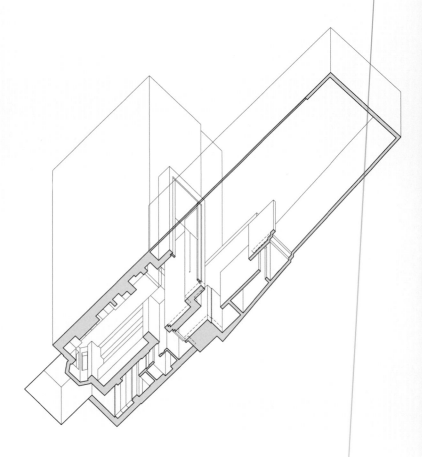

The Bed and The Bath

Placing the bathtub next to the underside of a basin, looking across at a WC, is an unsatisfactory arrangement. Moving the tub out of the bathroom and into the bedroom provides a more relaxing experience, with full-height folding and sliding doors allowing for several configurations, depending on the level of privacy required, and concealing the bathtub when not in use.

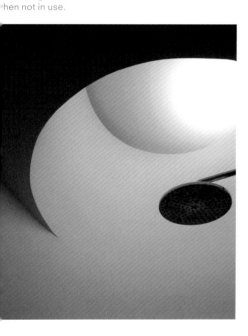

New-build three-storey house. Steel frame with concrete block walls and timber floors. White render and painted PVC mesh to exterior. Heated polished concrete floors to ground and basement. Dark stained oak floor to upper levels. Smooth plaster to walls and ceilings. Full-height flush pivoting doors. Frameless glazing and rooflights. Shot-blasted steel bookcases and fireplaces. Stainless steel kitchen. Ground source heat pump, photovoltaic panels and roof water collection system. 267m^2

House 9

Hampstead, London
Guard / Pollock, 2011

This new three-storey house in Hampstead incorporates an extensive glass facade. In order to prevent overlooking by neighbouring properties and to help control solar gain, external PVC mesh screens form an integral element of the facade and provide enclosure for external garden terraces. The open-plan living spaces unfold as a sequence of interlocking elements opening onto private courtyards at the front and back. The living spaces are arranged to take advantage of longer diagonal views looking over the garden landscape at the rear and along the street at the front. External gardens at first- and second-floor level are maintained by an automatic watering system fed by a rainwater collection tank at second-floor level. The galleried first floor and double-height reception room evoke the traditional London studio house, while the architectural detailing continues the strong tradition of modernist design in Hampstead.

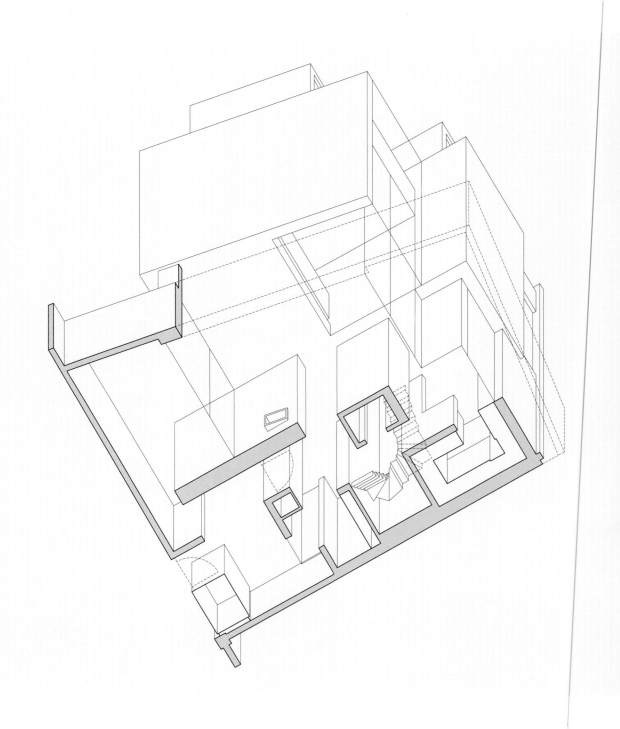

The Fabric Screen

The inclusion of extensive glass facades in a modern house can lead to a problem of privacy for the occupants, particularly if the house is in a built-up area and overlooked by neighbouring properties. To resolve the lack of privacy, and to help control solar gain, external PVC mesh screens act as huge net curtains. The occupants retain both light and privacy during the day without compromising views. A second skin of internal blinds provides conventional privacy at night.

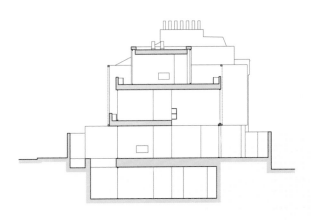

The Unbroken Surface

A tough polished concrete floor can provide a seamless connection between different functions and spaces, unifying the floor plane and forming an unbroken connection between inside and out. The utilitarian aesthetic forms a striking contrast and backdrop to the more delicate detailing and everyday objects of the domestic realm.

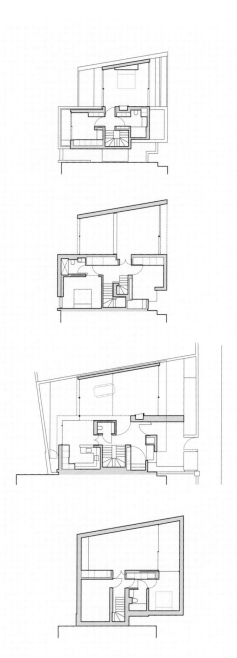

The Fragmented Garden

With the increasing density of inner city properties, the provision of individual garden spaces is difficult to achieve. In this particular house, the outdoor space is treated as a series of fragmented gardens, with courtyards at ground and basement level and terraces concealed behind the fabric screens, creating a walled garden effect on the upper floors.

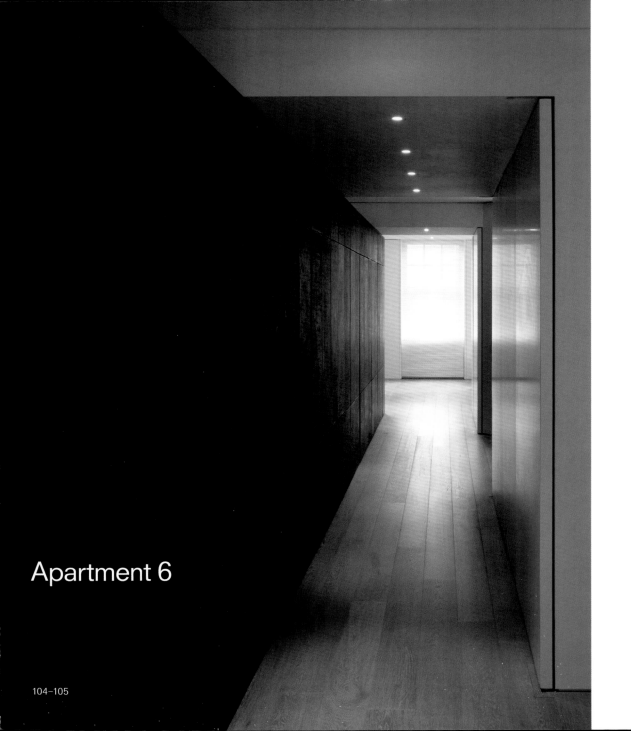

Apartment 6

Holland Park, London
Guard / Tillman / Mais, 2011

The late nineteenth-century mansion block introduced apartment living to London. This fifth-floor apartment originally contained an awkward, dark, winding central corridor that provided a distinct separation between rooms. From front to back, the apartment measured a generous 26 metres, yet there was no sense of this space. To simplify the plan and maximise the visual dimensions, a new storage wall was inserted along the full length of the apartment. Behind the black basalt-clad storage wall there are bathrooms, kitchens, guest bedrooms and an exercise space. This wall creates the apartment's 'spine'; a demarcation between public and private space without compromising the circulation flow through the rooms. The new formal route allows for a new connection between the living area on the north side with the south-facing master bedroom sitting area. If required, concealed full-height doors can transform this room into further en-suite guest accommodation.

Reconfigured fifth-floor apartment in mansion block. Oak flooring. White plaster to walls and ceilings. Full-height flush doors. Basalt storage wall. Limestone fireplace. Circular etched glass shower. 200m²

The Storage Wall

Services, storage and access are combined in a single central structure running practically the full length of the apartment. The black basalt cladding gives the spine storage wall a monumental, unified appearance, blurring the distinction between door and cupboard and preserving a public/private element to the space. Full-height pivoting doors can be folded across at various stages to subdivide the internal space.

Before

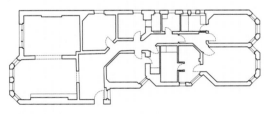

After

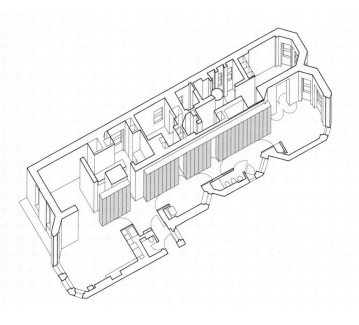

Highgate, London
Guard / Pollock, 2012

This new house was built on a landlocked site in north London. To access the property, it was necessary to create a driveway through the living room of an existing detached Victorian house. The new house is comprised of two interlocking boxes that form a covered entrance courtyard. The ground floor has a glazed facade looking out over the expansive woodland. The first-floor reception room has a projecting glass window that frames a stunning view over Queen's Wood and north-east London. The house exists in bucolic isolation yet is just five minutes from the London Underground.

New-build three-storey detached house. Steel and concrete frame. Concrete and metal stud walls. Polished concrete floors. Gravel entrance courtyard. Full-height doors and windows. Metal mesh and glass external terraces. Smooth plaster to walls and ceilings. Smooth natural render to exterior walls. Ground source heat pump. 268m²

House 10

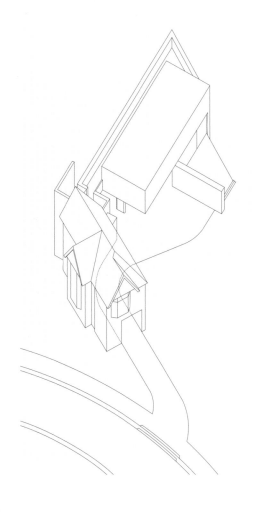

The Framed View

Unique settings and views can be given an architectural emphasis through the use of carefully placed and detailed windows. By setting the glazing out in front of the plane of the wall and concealing the window frame, the presence of the glass is diminished and the view brought into sharp focus.

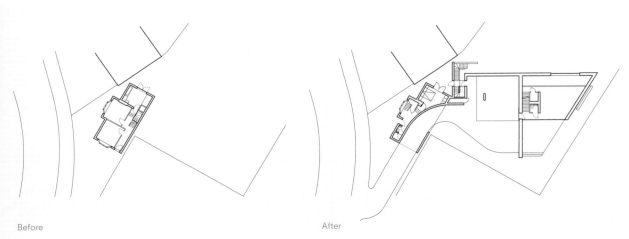

Before

After

The Abstracted Entrance

In the absence of a
street presence and
conventional front facade,
an entrance can become
more abstract and
exciting. With no windows
or conventional front
door to create a typical
domestic language, the
forms emphasise a more
mysterious and intriguing
character. The interior
qualities of the house
are kept concealed.

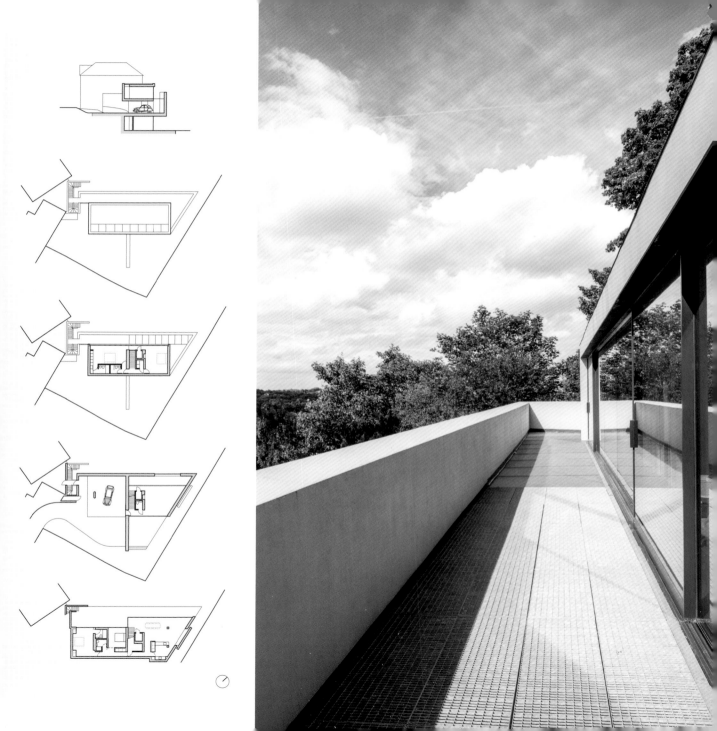

Maida Vale, London
Guard / Pollock, 2013

This extension to an Italianate villa in Maida Vale is separated from the main house by a glazed slot. The new modernist wing is arranged to allow the morning, afternoon and evening sunlight into the new kitchen and dining room. Internally, a glass bridge links the new extension to the upper ground-floor entrance hall, and the formal staircase is extended down to access the lower ground floor and the new basement below. The addition contains a new kitchen, double-height dining area and upper-floor study. Extensive use of rooflights brings light in from above and the side, and sliding glass panels open up the dining room to the large garden.

House 11

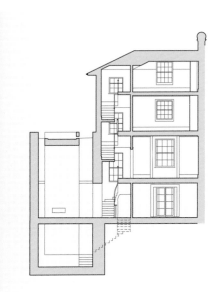

New extension to
refurbished semi-
detached Victorian house.
Concrete retaining walls
with steel frame and
rendered concrete block
external walls. Limestone
floor tiles. Stainless
steel kitchen. Concealed
sliding windows.
Frameless glass floors
and rooflights. Smart
glass. Smooth plaster to
walls and ceilings. 374m²

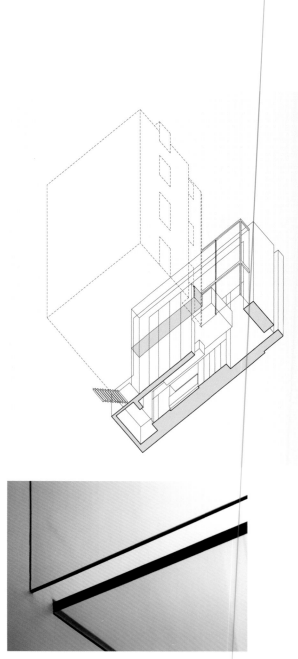

The Listed Building

The original form and
footprint of the listed house
is preserved by a glass
slot separating it from the
new side extension. In this
way, a clear distinction
is made between the
period detailing of the
original house and the new
extension, while the glass
slot introduces natural light
throughout the full length
of the new structure.

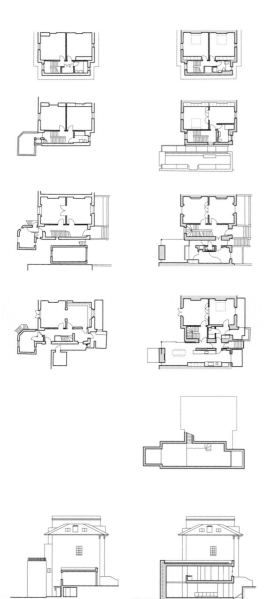

The Reflection of Sunlight

Sunlight is bounced off the south-west facing flank wall of the original house through the glass slot into the interior space. At certain times of the day and year, sunlight appears to come from two directions at once, creating an extraordinary effect throughout the interior (p 137).

Before   After

Maida Vale, London
Tillman, 2013

The existing top-floor maisonette in this elegant five-storey Victorian terrace house had a confused layout. The rearrangement of the space places the bedrooms and bathrooms on the lower floor and opens up the entire volume of the upper floor as a reception, dining, kitchen and study area. The sloping mansard walls of the upper floor are concealed behind new vertical storage that also conceals built-in shutters and sliding panels. An all-glass structural staircase links the sitting area to the study gallery above. A large skylight allows views from the study desk over the west London skyline. The main living space opens up to the west-facing terrace, extending the living space for dining in good weather.

Existing three-storey maisonette. Steel frame. Fumed oak floors. White plaster to walls and ceilings. Floor-to-ceiling pivoting and sliding doors. Frameless structural glass staircase. Purpose-designed Corian kitchen. Smart glass bathroom ceiling. 139m²

Apartment 7

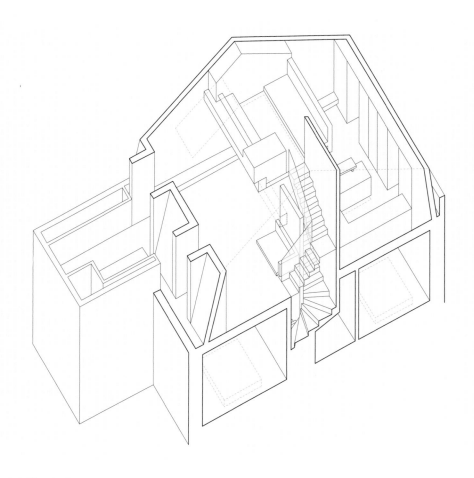

The Attic Disguised

Attic spaces with mansard walls can have a certain charm. However, for a formal living space, the vertical wall is an important element. Vertical panels concealing useful storage disguise the slope of the mansard roof, while strong horizontal and vertical forms overcome any feeling of being relegated to what was originally a secondary space.

The Low Ceiling

Due to space restraints it is often necessary to have a lower floor-to-ceiling height. This does not have to feel claustrophobic. Instead, by ensuring the proximity of intimate spaces and larger volumes, a strong hierarchy of use is created, with a sense of perspective and familiarity generated by the views from one to another.

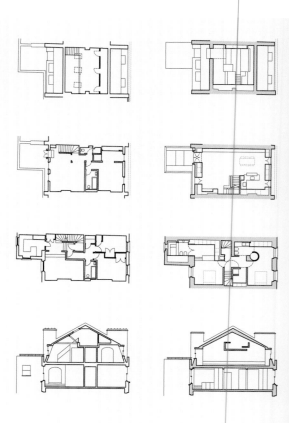

Before

After

House 12

Benirrás, Ibiza
Guard / Tillman / Pollock, 2015

New-build two-storey detached house. Steel and concrete construction. Hollow clay block walls. White rendered exterior. Microcement floors throughout. Smooth plaster to walls and ceilings. Floor-to-ceiling sliding glazed panels. Solar water heating panels. 431m²

Sat high in the hills next to wild woodlands, this new house takes its inspiration from the hill farms of northern Ibiza, where gradual additions by different generations have created an informal arrangement of buildings and courtyards. Planned on a 4.5-metre grid to suit the maximum size of a one-piece double-glazed window unit, the new house is arranged so that all the motorised floor-to-ceiling windows can slide into wall pockets. In good weather, the house is effectively windowless, transformed into a series of covered spaces and removing any distinction between inside and out. The house is arranged to cool itself passively with cross ventilation, ponds and opening rooflights. The windows are positioned to take advantage of the stunning 180-degree views over the northern Ibizan terrain, with the living space looking north-west towards a distant sea view framed by hills. A sunken outside sitting area with fireplace takes advantage of the setting sun.

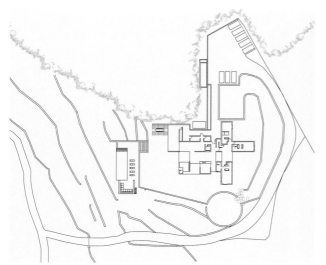

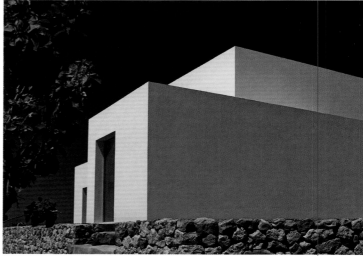

The Aligned View

Detached country houses
in cool climates are
traditionally orientated
to take advantage of
the sun. In hot climates,
sunlight needs to be
controlled, allowing for
other orientations to be
prioritised. Arranging
windows and alignments
to exploit certain key views
can help to create a strong
sense of place and location,
as well as orientate the
interior arrangement.

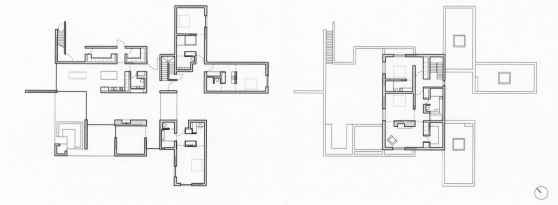

The Disappearing Window

Warm climates present the interesting opportunity to live without glass and create a seamless connection between inside and outside, from shadow to sunlight with cool breezes. At night or in winter, motorised floor-to-ceiling glass panels slide out from hollow pockets contained in the external walls to enclose the interior as required.

The Gentle Breeze

The walls of the ground-floor bedrooms create a courtyard offering relief from the sun. A pond separating the living area from the courtyard reflects the morning sunlight, creating dappled reflections on the ceiling of the living space. Sliding the motorised single sheet glass panels back into the wall pockets allows the prevailing eastern summer breeze to pass through the courtyard, over the pond and through the house to cool the internal temperature.

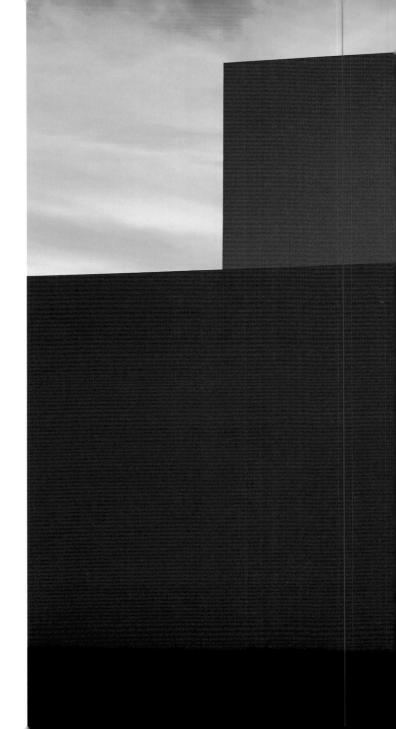

Reflections

The internal finishes used in most of the projects in this book are hard materials. Floors are timber, stone or concrete. Walls and ceilings are smooth plaster and are painted white or off-white to reflect light. Doors and cupboards are full-height and flush with the walls. Glass, whether used for rooflights or balustrades, has concealed fixings. To achieve a simple and perhaps more basic sense of enclosure, skirtings, architraves and cornices are omitted. Removing traditional detail and acknowledging the power of the straight line creates an abstracted neutral backdrop for furniture, art and possessions. Light from above is brought into the home through the double-height space and the rooflight. Placing a rooflight or window next to a wall allows slow-moving shafts of sunlight to fall across a flat plane, enhancing our well-being through a connection to a more fundamental existence. Embracing views and welcoming natural light can form three-dimensional spaces full of shadows and silhouettes that change throughout the day, varying with the weather and the seasons. As property becomes increasingly expensive there is a need for smaller, more affordable homes that are appropriate for denser urban environments and contemporary city life. A simple aesthetic approach, incorporating multifunctional spaces, generous storage and daylight from above, can create homes that are both efficient and spacious, homes that provide us with a calm environment to allow a better perspective on our lives and the complex world around us

Mark Perrott Guard, 2016

Photography

Acknowledgements

The partners would like to acknowledge the help of both Eva Jiřičná and the late Rick Mather in the early days of the architectural practice. We would also like to acknowledge the important role played by our former associate, Charles Barclay, in the studio's first works, and to thank Georgie Wolton for her valuable contribution to several key projects. Ryan Bainbridge and Gavin Ramsey spent essential time preparing and updating the project information while Jonathan Bell and Tim George have been extremely encouraging and supportive throughout the whole process of producing the book.

All the projects in this book are the result of a team effort and the partners would like to thank all those who have contributed to the work of the studio over the years. In particular, our consultant structural engineers require special recognition for their help and inventive solutions to the many complexities that have been encountered in these projects. We would also like to thank the contractors and the many subcontractors who have made each project a success. Finally, we would like to thank our clients for their support, patience and understanding. Without them these projects could not have been achieved.

Studio:

Tom Appels
Ryan Bainbridge
Teresa Barry
Andrew Brownless
George Bunkall
Simon Chadwick
Tony Chan
Robert Cullen
Marco Curtaz
Michael Delaney
Stephen Downes
Kat Dray
Bosco Fair
David Grunberg
Stephan Haensler
Jonathan Harris
Grant Hutchinson
Akpesiri Iyovwaye
Richard Keep
Sean Koudela

Mary Lee-Woolf
Tomasz Lelen
Jason Mais
Elaine Manalo
Chris Procter
Gavin Ramsey
Neil Randall
Rui Ribeiro
David Sacks
Lukasz Sadura
Tomas Skocek
Tom Sharp
Nicholas Stickland
Philip Tebbutt
Niel du Toit
Felicity Toop
Simon Walker
Amelia Ward
Hsien Wong
Daniel Woolfson

Structural Engineers:

Michael Baigent Orla Kelly Ltd
Michael Chester & Partners
Dewhurst Macfarlane & Partners
Fidler Associates
Fluid Structures Ltd
Hugh Griffin Associates

Quantity Surveyors:

Baillie Knowles Partnership
Burr & Neve
Peter Henderson Associates
Stockdale

Consultants:

David Brooke Consulting
Norman England
Eta Projects
David Maycox & Co
Sandy Brown Associates
Mike Sindic

Contractors:

Amega Contracts Ltd
Ashcon Construction Ltd
Andy Barcoe
Chalk Hill Construction Ltd
Kevin Clack
Claremont Construction Ltd
Creative Craftsmen Ltd
Cuddy Development Ltd
Delcon Construction Ltd
Ethos Construction Solutions Ltd
Goodford Contractors Ltd
Harris Calnan Construction Ltd
Innerspace
Neil Lawrence & Co
Metrotech
Sandproyect SL
Sherlock Interiors Contracting Ltd
Varbud Construction Co Ltd
RG & M Wadlow & Son Ltd
Chong Yeoh

Guard Tillman Pollock consists of a small team of architects interested in the development of elegant, functional modernist design. The studio specialises in the development of transformable spaces that combine space, light and form with flexible living accommodation. The brief is carefully analysed in close consultation with the client and the final design is arrived at by establishing the essential components, to which a richness of function is then added. The practice works closely with contractors and fabricators to achieve technical advances within the industry, and a strong architectural approach has led to modernist solutions being accepted and approved by planning and conservation groups. Through lateral thought and the analysis of function, the partners believe better solutions to old problems can be found.

Pictured left to right: Steven Pollock, Mark Perrott Guard and Keith Tillman in the meeting room at the Whitfield Street Studio, July 2016.

Guard Tillman Pollock

© 2017 Artifice books on architecture, the editors and the authors. All rights reserved.

Artifice books on architecture
10A Acton Street
London
WC1X 9NG

t. +44 (0)207 713 5097
f. +44 (0)207 713 8682
sales@artificebooksonline.com
www.artificebooksonline.com

ISBN 978-1-911339-03-8

British Library Cataloguing-in-Publication Data. A CIP record for this book is available from the British Library.

Design: Tim George
Typeface: Neuzeit Grotesk

Artifice books on architecture is an environmentally responsible company. *Walls and Boxes: Guard Tillman Pollock* is printed on sustainably sourced paper.